OBSERVATIONS OF LIFE

ONE LINE AT A TIME

*Soon-to-Be-Famous Quotes
From a Not-So-Famous Person*

Neil McClure

Observations of Life ~ One Line at a Time: Soon-To-Be Famous Quotes from a Not-So-Famous Person

Copyright © 2017 by Neil McClure

ISBN: 978-0-692-99302-6

Editor: Debra Jason;   Cover/Interior Design: Peggy Sands;   Cover Photo: Ken Sanville

This book is a work of fiction. Names, phases, quotations, characters, businesses, organizations, places, events and incidents either are the product of the author's imagination or are used fictitiously. Any resemblance to actual persons, living or dead, events, locales, or other published phases and quotations is entirely coincidental.

Printed in the United States of America.

Printed by CreateSpace, An Amazon.com Company

Available from Amazon.com and other retail outlets

First Edition

2 4 6 8 10

For additional copies or information contact: neil@observationsoflife.com

Send me
a comment!

Dedication

This book was born from the world around us. So naturally I owe gratitude to the world in its entirety. Inspiration for these quotes came from every corner of my life, from loved ones to strangers, business associates to competitors, and our general societal efforts to improve life that is balanced by the absurdity in the world.

Primary thanks for inspiration are owed to all those who have been a part of my life over the last 15 years. Some people just passed through it, while others remain tolerant of me. To Diana, who inspired the start of this list of observations; to all the people at Hart InterCivic; to my lifelong friend Casey; and to Lisa, who loved me and transitioned me from engineer to author.

Thank you to my family: sisters Meredith and Marta, children Shanley and Davis who continue to encourage me to hope for the world, their mother Wendy, and my mom Peggy. Many others of you may recognize quotes and the shared laughter of those moments that are memorialized within these pages. You all brought me joy and now I hope our time brings some measure of entertainment to the rest of the world. I thank you all for being a part of my life.

Lastly, to the late Ed McClure, who never understood my career path in relation to the 37 years he spent with the same company. My dad was unaware he had enabled my professional choices through the experiences he gave me during my upbringing. I believe he eventually 'got it' and passed away being proud of his son, something I was grateful to give back to him. A classic "Greatest Generation" father, I only hope I've become as good a man as he was and have given my children as much as he gave me.

Introduction

Have you ever had a conversation with someone where you say something, then stop and think, "Whoa, that sounded pretty good/funny/profound/poetic/deep"? That's what this book is — a compilation of those moments in life.

In 2003, I was at my desk working, doing the management thing, talking to an employee and made a comment to illustrate a point to her. She left and I thought, "Hmmm, what did I just say?" I wrote it down on a Post-it® note which became number one on the list and the start of a new pile of notes on my desk.

Over the next couple of months, I added more Post-it notes to the pile as I found it entertaining. At some point, I repeated the latest Post-it note to a co-worker. A short time later, she sent me an e-mail with the quote (number 27 on the list) emblazoned on a presentation slide along with graphics she had added to it, making it look suspiciously like the "Home Sweet Home" embroidered wall hanging. I then entered all the Post-it notes to date in a document and began a list entitled "Needlepoint Patterns for the New Millennium". The title evolved from there to become what it is today after twelve different possibilities.

Over time, I became more attentive and more disciplined at writing quotes down before they vanished into the noise of the day. I started writing them on the back of my business cards and collecting these words of wisdom from all aspects of my life, including business, home, parenting, relationships and other areas where nonsense and laughter occurred. I became more prolific and it was the first time I ran out of business cards before my title changed!

As the list grew, so did the document on my laptop. Having spent most of my career in product development, I understood the value of user feedback. I was traveling a lot through 2008 and my favorite time for user input was on an airplane when seated next to a personable passenger. I'd pull up the document and randomly pick a page and we'd read through a dozen or so. I discovered that people were entertained by the list and started thinking about creating a book.

I discussed the development of the book with professionals in various industries, including publishing. They offered up suggestions related to re-ordering, categorizing, explaining and accompanying with illustrations to help the user understand the quotes. In the end, I decided to let the quotes stand on their own. They are listed and numbered based on the order in which each was created. There is no grouping by theme – you never know what the next one will be about. There is no explanation or illustration – you must interpret each one based on your own life experiences. (Some may not have meaning for you until the next day, after sleeping on it!)

As far as I know, these quotes are all original material; I have not copied, borrowed or otherwise included anything quoted by anyone else. Undoubtedly, others may have quoted something similar with the same intent, but not worded the same or included as part of this type of collection. Sure, I've had lots of help from those who've passed through my life, mostly as inspiration and occasionally with word selection to fit on one line. Any similarity to published statements by other (famous) people is purely coincidental and unintentional.

—————

~ I hope you have as much fun reading this book as I have had creating it! ~

VOLUME I

*The following quotes are a sampling from over
3,000 that I have created over the last 15 years.*

The quotes for Volume I were chosen primarily at random and I tried to avoid numerically successive quotes for some unknown reason. In the final editing, there were quotes removed that I really wanted to share, but I ran out of room. If Volume I creates any measure of an audience, the missing numbered quotes will appear in future volumes. And the list continues to grow…

1. An unexpected response uncovers hidden opportunity

5. You can make assumptions but not raise expectations

8. Behind every reason is a purpose

12. Don't let temperature interfere with attitude

13. A lot of shit is just a crapshoot

15. It's always easier to edit than create

19. If we knew what we were doing, we'd never get anything done

22. The position of the cart and horse is irrelevant in the information age

23. The net present value of trust is risk

25. Enjoy an expert in anything

27. The only reality about theory is that it is never the same in practice

28. Don't be encumbered by thoughts of preparation

31. Some of these are better than others

33. Don't rise to the blame equation

35. Your accusation is not my admission

38. Career path is the coincidental alignment with corporate objectives

41. One man's safety is another woman's fears

43. You can't judge a man's TV addiction by the size of his screen

48. Assessments of normalcy require a reference

54. Take a breath before you respond

55. Know when to instigate versus mitigate

59. When you least expect it – an unknown sporting event

60. If you eat eggs, you're pro-choice

66. Their opinions will come and go but your decisions are here to stay

69. Heed the cycles of emotional imbalance

72. Sometimes it's just better to go in blind

76. We're not sure what we're building and it's already late

77. Adjust your view, cars are just an appliance

80. Don't combine drugs in a single conversation

82. While nostril hair can be a distraction, continue your train of thought

84. If it was a placebo, I need a stronger one

94. When shopping for a woman, go for something that doesn't have to fit

99. Science once again fails under the weight of politics

104. There's a lot of validity in low expectations

107. There are dreams and then there are actions on beliefs

109. Attitude is the best diet

115. An excess of anything will harm you

117. If somebody isn't upset with you, you're not doing anything

125. Obsolescence generally arrives before end of life

129. Everybody is in some stage of therapy

133. Too often, humor is in the eye of the originator

139. Perpetual annoyance is not a mood swing

149. The best you'll ever be is the day after you left

151. Let it fail on its own, don't wish it to death

155. You can't have too many twisted friends, just not all at once

162. In attempts to be funny, sometimes it isn't

165. Power cycling is not a user feature

167. A selection of one is not a choice

173. Be tough, be proud, live lonely

176. A love of lifestyles overshadows professional dissatisfaction

183. Chasing your dreams can be lonely at times

187. Engineering is about logic, politics is without

189. The people who don't know, suspect

191. They'll never do it same the way you would

193. Big girl, good dog, bad bunny

200. Your efficiencies are my annoyance

206. Relish it while you have enough mustard

211. Always be susceptible to a reasonable argument

213. Delude yourself with confidence and the rest will follow

219. The abuse is always tougher when the effort is volunteered

222. If you're going to talk to yourself, listen

224. If you have to explain it, you've failed to communicate

228. Driving is a social event so quit picking your nose

241. Put off today what you can detonate tomorrow

248. Men are all boys and girls are all moms

250. That's the problem with opportunity - it never shows up as imagined

254. Our calendar is based on the menstrual cycle

263. Good ideas can be poorly applied

278. It's pretty complicated to be yourself

280. Most of what your kids learn from you is unintentional

284. All the reasons you want to be with me are the ones that drive you crazy

290. One accident away from going nowhere all day

307. What was once tolerable is now annoying

323. Sober people in a panic are worse than drunks with no worries

327. A woman can do it all but a man can only do so much

336. Everyone is creative but not everyone will take the risk

342. My nature is to make your life dangerous

369. I just want to remain reasonably current in your memory

373. There's always less of your life to live in

392. If it happens by accident, it will be really convenient

398. As you get older, remember to take the rebel out for a ride

400. The only thing kids give back while growing up are viruses

408. The emotional pendulum swings at equal amplitude in both directions

410. A relationship with flight attendants should never leave the plane

424. Be willing to give up some control for the sake of entertainment

429. If your argument sucks, say it louder and wave your hands a lot

432. I outperform my powers of recovery

442. When you don't have the money, you have the time

448. If it doesn't make sense, there's something else going on

453. Rather than worrying about saving, just stop spending

464. I can be this lonely without you

471. It's something I constantly try to avoid with marginal success

493. I'm sure it's because I didn't do something that you didn't ask

498. Just because you've giving up responsibility doesn't mean I've assumed any

513. Motion gives the illusion of output

517. You can lose the marbles but not the keys

528. No rest for the competent

553. As with most people, I'm equally surprised by what comes out of my mouth

560. People will always criticize your decisions, so don't be afraid to make them

568. Trophy wives for second place are less demanding

579. If you raise them, you never let go of the known faults

580. For men it's an opportunity but with women it's a choice

593. If you have problems without money, don't win the lottery

599. You can blame all you want but you're the reason you're unhappy

602. She's reasonably safe but I like to promote her dangerous side

609. I not laughing, I'm just enjoying your concern

611. Prepare to be an errant parent

632. Being technically challenged results in a longer life expectancy

646. In a house with five women, the roll never stops spinning

648. People do change but it's more often physical than psychological

657. As you get older, the correct fluids are essential

670. Being right is way overrated

692. Women don't understand directions and men don't read them

701. If you don't get along in the vertical position, the horizontal won't work

713. Intermittent reinforcement beats periodic annoyance

735. Sacrificing a virgin is such a waste

738. Figure out your enablers and keep them happy

741. The advantage of being married is that you always have somebody to blame

757. Make them do it while they're still minors

762. I'm a safety guy in a risky environment

769. I'm not enriched by deep conversations with people I don't know

777. The only thing he's invented is a way to word it

781. I don't need to be measured, I get enough competition from myself

793. Your life experiences are just one obstructed view after another

800. It's never the people you know, it's the ones they know

806. You've been stretching the truth so long it's lost all its elasticity

811. If it ever has anything to do with your china, something is terribly wrong

816. While that's not like me, there are certainly many examples

822. If you ask me for feedback, my comments are not wrong

826. I've done stupid things that were planned

830. "But it was half off" is not an accounting term

835. If it depends on who you know, you'll always need them

845. Avoid being a victim of your own expectations

851. Help, I've forgotten my glasses and can't read my list

858. Double-checking for the first time is after the fact

877. Silently let me know without any obvious indication

880. The only fit for the reasonable-man standard is a woman

884. Self-ass kicking is exhausting

886. It's not easy being me with you

888. It would be satisfying just to hold her attention

893. Shooting blanks is different than just missing

907. I miss you but nothing else around you

920. Principles are fine but don't invoke them when you're paying hourly rates

938. Plumber-butt nothing, that was the whole sewer system

944. Getting motivated is a constant effort

951. You've only learned the lesson if you don't repeat the mistake

954. Live large and pass out early

959. I can't remember what I haven't been told

970. Courage and stupidity are often difficult to distinguish

974. When you take yourself too seriously, you're defenseless against humor

986. The only way to herd cats is down a hallway

991. Fantasies of success are rarely accompanied by nightmares of effort

1001. Willpower and inspiration are unreliable

1003. It's a good thing I'm present to laugh at my own jokes

1008. Even bad news is good information

1010. My light is never on but somebody is generally home

1014. People with complaints are not hard to find

1018. Sometimes I just can't figure out how to make her right

1038. Any guy that wears a sun visor probably wants to carry a purse

1042. Never underestimate the value of reminders

1046. You do your thing and we'll do around you

1048. I'm a one person case study

1055. What a terrible burden to always know everything

1064. You can check my genes but should probably stay away from my shorts

1066. I'll claim to be ignorant as soon as I can get away with it

1069. A guy considers half-naked to be divided at the waist

1074. Some days are just limited to maintaining your balance

1084. 60 is the new 50 unless you acted 20 when you were 40

1098. If you can't handle criticism, keep your mouth shut

1105. If it wasn't so disgusting, it would be pretty impressive

1107. There are times when a total lack of control requires discipline

1108. The only thing needed for an opportunity is the courage to take it

1115. Nice guys exist – they just stay hidden to keep safe

1116. When holding on to principles, prepare to sleep in uncomfortable places

1127. Let it go when the need to be right makes you miserable

1129. A woman in control has room for surrender

1135. If you're not going to be invited back, stay as long as you can

1141. If I'm not looking at you when I say it, don't be offended when you hear it

1155. My level of malice is balanced only by my degree of ambivalence

1166. Try getting out in front of your dreams instead of following them

1175. If we always agree, one of us is lying

1180. Be careful what you threaten

1188. Sharp tools save time – especially English

1195. I found everything I need and it amounted to nothing

1199. When I give you the space you request, you can't hold it against me

1201. I need to keep finding ways to fuel your apprehension

1205. My thoughts of you are chivalrous with embellishments of sensory stimulation

1212. Is a guy still an asshole if there is nobody around to piss off

1226. I'm an ADD stalker – I'll follow for only a little while

1230. Girls start out good and boys start out nice

1237. There's what you'd like to do and then there's the time you have

1240. Sorry, I really meant to look at your eyes

1255. It's costing a lot if the cones are set out and orange vests are involved

1257. Things aren't too bad with a glass half empty position, bone-dry sucks

1276. Go ahead and be right, I just won't be around to celebrate your victory

1284. Most times, what they ask for isn't what they want

1286. None of us are as impressed with you as you are with yourself

1290. The biggest problem is I don't remember what's wrong with my memory

1292. The gap between mental and physical age continues to widen as you grow older

1294. Old guys are haunted by phantom menstrual cycles

1297. If you don't really know, state it with confidence

1307. Marriage is just an act and has nothing to do with the effort

1312. Curiosity maimed the human

1315. In all honesty, I am sincere

1317. Does atheism require practicing

1319. I could be high maintenance if I could find somebody to perform it

1321. Daughters don't let dads wear Speedos

1323. Its practical to engage a girl and her dog but stay away from her little brother

.

1332. I hope I've already had my 15 minutes of fame

1348. If your new look is always better than the last, keep the same friends

1350. It's not a good idea if a known result is diarrhea

1354. I'm not that smart, I just make things up with confidence

1357. Consistency forces me to do a lot of things I would have given up years ago

1365. Life is challenging and then you become one

1376. The little things only count if you turn them into big issues

1392. Success is often balanced by destructive behavior

1397. Never ever say never, never, ever

1399. I'll only behave if we use my definition

1409. Why argue with your perceptions

1410. Everybody was born with one and then some add another through marriage

1416. I hate it when I bet against myself and lose

1418. If you don't survive your heart attack, you don't have to exercise after it

1424. Your girlfriend can be much younger based on your money or her weight

1435. Everybody dies with it still being a mystery

1438. Beliefs guide your actions, assumptions manage your emotions

1440. Being wise is no guarantee that you'll exercise wisdom

1446. Just another bad dad joke

1451. Quality is not established by cost

1456. There's a difference between being supportive and taking a side

1458. I can't even agree with you without getting in trouble

1461. It will all eventually work out but time is the critical variable

1465. Quit giving me eyebrow attitude

1469. I can't make you happy forever but I could entertain you for a while

1472. Do you need to correct their English if you know it's a lie

1477. Even shooting blanks still causes trouble

1482. If you're the one who thinks it should get done, do it without complaint

1487. They're not secrets, they're undiscovered history

1489. I'm beginning to consider the possibility of being optimistic

1499. I want to have a longer relationship with my daughter than with my mother

1503. The harder you fight the funk, the longer it lasts

1506. I won't hold it against you, I'll just bring it back around

1510. Getting organized is a lifelong effort

1516. I'm tired of good excuses

1522. Thank you for letting me entertain myself at my expense

1525. I always knew where I was going, I just didn't know when

1526. An offer is unconditional but a request is subject to scheduling

1529. Anybody who has a peg board doesn't really use his tools

1530. If you tell them not to, it's license to

1532. If you're entertained wherever you are, it doesn't matter where you go

1550. I ♥ Haters

1562. It's never one thing after another, it's a bunch of crap all at once

1571. The key to aging gracefully is increased medical procedures and substance abuse

1578. Never assume you are a clear communicator

1584. There is no such thing as an empty nest with an adolescent spouse

1586. Claiming innocence leaves me guilty

1602. The only way to beat the breast obsession is to have a pair

1604. When pointing to encourage focus, use two fingers

1628. I'll never know how you feel, so you'll always have to tell me

1635. I like nice places where I can behave badly

1641. You are responsible for my trust in you

1645. There is a difference between a wedgie and a thong

1647. How can you ever be smart if you don't do anything stupid

1651. You hear way more than I say

1656. You don't know more when you get older, you just get more obstinate

1661. The minimum baggage we all carry is maternal

1667. If you wait for the right time, it will be too late

1674. Many lifelong dreams become nightmares when finally lived out

1676. Once you pass calculus, start working on your English

1702. You should say that again because you need to hear it more

1723. There are a great many mysteries in the world and most involve women

1727. I don't need to be right but you are so wrong

1729. If you keep your expectations low, you'll always be happy

1731. Coarse desires result in irritated satisfaction

1743. Your interest won't change but your tolerance may vary

1745. If you have breakfast for dinner, you can get up at noon

1755. I have nothing to gain by making you look bad

1759. If you're better now, I'm glad I didn't know you then

1762. Change doesn't change unless accompanied by accomplishment

1767. There's no better revenge than accepting what you loathe

1771. Eventually, a low probability event will occur that changes your life forever

1778. I have nothing to hide so you'll have to live with any discovery

1783. It's a shame we vote for who we don't want

1788. Everyone has flaws when placed under a microscope

1791. When fighting for your life, don't plan beyond your next move

1797. Decisions by women are driven by different motivations than men

1802. Use a higher pitch for bitching and lower one for scolding so I know the difference

1808. I'm the last to know and the one who cares the least

1816. Knowing what happened is nice but "how" has the real value

1822. If you show up with nothing, it doesn't matter if it's guns or knives

1834. I know who you are better than I remember what you did

1836. Severance pay is spring break for adults

1850. The future needs to arrive so it can become the past

1852. I'm actually a simple person but a complex guy

1862. I need your help with what you need

1865. Hope is not a retirement plan

1872. An AARP card is a license to forget

1874. I can make dinner, but I'm not fixing any entrées

1876. I'm glad you only ask for things that you already have

1882. There is nothing that I need from you other than what you give

1887. Preparing for the transition will bring on the change

1892. There is always uncertainty until the moment of occurrence

1896. You can always find a job that nobody else wants

1901. People are like cars when they get older because it's OK to leak a few fluids

1906. What I lack in height I make up for in vascularity

1908. An inventor never dies, he just makes up things that don't work

1910. I'll worry no matter what you choose, the worries will just be different

1914. It's often hard to maintain confidence while exercising patience

1919. You can't return the value of an unconditional gift

1928. You believe your intuition is infallible to validate your insecurities

1931. The biggest liar demands the greatest truth

1934. Like is the operational component of love

1942. Trust is not a binary measure

1944. I want to love and the random collisions of the universe brought me you

1960. Lies and deceit will imprison you to loneliness and isolation

1963. It's alright to be a helper but caretakers need to go

1967. Males are twisted and women just men straight

1970. Man caves are a result of boy burrows

1978. I want to tonight but I wish I didn't in the morning

1979. The lesser of two evils needs a third choice

1985. I live frugally but support extravagant events

1996. I rely on what you tell me, so do what you say

2007. It's healthy to get an occasional reminder of what zero ambition looks like

2014. A sober desire transforms into an intoxicated need

2019. If making it better makes it more complicated, it ends up worse

2020. The afternoon was really fun which is why I'm texting an apology

2026. Not knowing what you want only means you're open to different possibilities

2032. Together we're just different but separately we're weird

2044. You can bite off an ear but you should never eat the whole bunny

2047. I invited you in without hesirvation

2058. Sometimes people come into your life to highlight what you need to be aware of

2064. I have balance in my life, it's just not centered

2066. Hostile Hospitality

2071. Nothing is ever that intentional because it would require focused intent

2074. There's always the possibility for you to lose additional control

2080. The sad part is that I could actually live up to the rumors

2089. No one person can know it all but many claim it

2091. Holding babies is better than operating heavy equipment

2094. Yes, we all have unique gifts and it's a shame that mine are so obscure

2098. It would be tough to be someone around you

2101. Just when I think there is no hope for you, you remind me there isn't

2105. Your pattern in relationships appears to be random

2109. I prefer the low pitch permission over the high pitch rejection

2121. Accidents are the same as unintentional actions

2123. Life is a series of random reactions that seem best for you at the time

2127. Attention Deficit Disorder is simply high speed changes of priorities

2132. A good place to picnic is under the shady section of the family tree

2136. If you admit you're wrong, you'll get your way more often

2138. Doctors, lawyers, accountants...I have a machinist on my contact list

2141. I'm not afraid to fail, which makes me fearless

2145. She would run out of time in a time travel movie

2151. Slips, trips and falls can be the result of leaks, drips and spills

2158. I'd be interested in erectifying your self esteem

2165. Everything you bitched at me about is the way you treated me

2169. I like you on your best misbehavior

2172. There is no sense hoping that I'll guess what you want

2175. Anything that requires a lifetime of practice is unattainable

.

2181. I may look suspicious but I'm still trustworthy

2185. I want to get cremated to save my children the cost of shipping and storage

2193. You can't win an argument about the way I feel

2198. The 'not like I used to' list grows faster than your age

2200. Counting days before your drug test is as effective as the Catholic rhythm method

2205. Nothing worse than arguing over who was wrong and losing the argument

2211. I prefer a job with no description

2213. Don't bitch at me about your guilt

2217. I can't tell if she's wearing me out or using me up

2225. Responsible hoarding is limiting your storage space to a single shopping cart

2236. Emptying your pockets should include small change, washers and a pair of nuts

2241. Shoot for the moon and settle for a low earth orbit

2246. Flight attendants meet more assholes than waitresses

2248. I don't understand women who hang with a guy wearing a man-bun

2252. It's hard to find a woman who will take the blame right away

2258. Fracking gas holes

2262. Exercising your rights is not required, any individual can give them up

2267. It's too easy to find penises on the internet without any friends

2270. I've been saying "I'll know better the next time" all of my life

2275. The advocates never proclaim the 'right to your life'

2279. I hate the fact that I'm still learning hard lessons

2283. If I paid attention, I'd know that you don't

2287. Quit giving it away for free and expecting payment later

2290. If there is nothing in your peripheral vision, everything is in front of you

2292. I need a woman who gets injured if I'm not there to protect her

2297. There should be a consequence for your ignorance

2302. Forget the maintenance expense, I can't even afford the acquisition cost

2309. If you're a little more than cock-eyed, you're just being a dick head

2321. We have no itinerary and we're sticking with that plan

2323. Do not try to be responsible for my happiness because you'll screw it up every time

2327. When you're far enough away, a wave or the finger looks the same

2329. No, you have to work your ass off for decades before you can do what I do

2336. I don't need to see your buttons to push them

2339. I have enough antibodies to be with you

2344. Everything happens for a reason and I just wish I knew what it was

2355. Make all the wrong decisions you want, just don't fuck up somebody else's life

2364. I want you to know that it only really, really, really bothers me a little bit

2367. Occasional indulgences do not have lasting impact

2370. If they don't react the way you expect, you won't like them

2375. Jokes are like business strategies, sometimes they don't work

2379. The shortcomings of technology always arrive at the human interface

2381. Real friends allow all debts to be even

2389. It's alright if they see you looking, just don't let them hear you talking

2394. Some people use a rabbit's foot but I carry a lucky wiener

2397. Self-Destruct-O Man – the only super hero that doesn't need an arch villain

2399. I can't even tell you how much I don't like that approach

2401. Don't let the fear of rejection prevent you from contributing something creative

2404. Anybody successful hears the words but understands the body language

2410. No argument you provide will ever change the mind of your critics

2415. I'd much rather have something about me go viral than virus

2420. Same old shit, different age

2427. I don't hit a home run every time but neither do MLB players

2432. Software is unable to fix processes that don't make sense

2436. The second quickest way to a woman's heart is through your tools

2441. Try to fall in love every day

2446. I'm not a big fan of dogs the size of cats

~ Neil McClure ~

2458. Worry offers no solitude from your problems

2460. Accidently getting pregnant happens to both the young and old

2465. Whether you talk to me or not, I'm still acting in your best interest

2468. Learn to say no at work and you'll be much better at your job

2477. I've never understood the appeal of non-consensual sex

2481. You can only earn loyalty through commitment

2488. I used to think I was handicapped as an engineer but then I met an attorney

2490. You don't have to feel guilty about the choices I make

2497. Never try to drink using the hand that holds the leash

2500. We've known each other for a long time, we just hadn't met yet

2506. It was recommended by a stranger with no interests similar to mine

2508. I didn't have a problem with it, I have experience at not laughing

2516. The world would be a better place if wealth wasn't handed down

2521. You should never have a good answer for the limitations in your life

2524. You came here looking for the best so don't complain about the cost

2529. Your problems seem like the worst until you hear about someone else's

2533. It's good that you didn't mind because I didn't care

2540. Anything you try to do for my happiness takes away from it

2545. I know you're lonely because you're not with me

2550. She doesn't use many facial expressions but she sure gestures a lot

2558. I can judge and pass it regularly

2563. I'd much rather hear a foul mouth than see a pursed lip

2569. I love hair color that's dyed and gone to heaven

2582. I'm right but will say you are

2585. The average amount is too much for her and not enough for him

2588. You're free to listen when I talk to myself but you can't ask any questions

2593. I've had Olympic performances many times but not in any supported sport

2596. I don't care about anything other than how you feel about it

2599. I'd say "don't do anything I wouldn't do" except it wouldn't rule anything out

2604. In order to create a family, relationships will be tested

2614. Dogs don't care if you're late as long as you show up

2626. I get distracted by people in front of me, it's easier if they're in the mirror

2629. Some people never seem to get anything done and spend a lot time doing it

2637. You can have the right question but ask it at the wrong time

2640. Lucky your woman isn't an earthquake since you're always activating her faults

2648. I can make wherever I am fun, except court

2654. Thinking of someone and wishing them wellness and peace is the same as prayer

2661. I prefer slow maintenance over low

2665. Some people exercise to stay in shape and others do it to change it

2676. There is someone in this world unlike anything you can think of

2679. That's for me to say and for you not to agree with

2684. I've learned long ago to let go of great ideas

2687. Of all the probability available, we should never be surprised by a single story

2691. The walking dead are real and were created by the pharmaceutical companies

2693. If she ever says she just wet her pants, ask which fluids she used

2697. First impressions matter in business

2705. If you listen to what angry people say, sometimes you can take it away from them

2709. It's best to operate with a preference reference

2712. You're busy when they're young and they're busy when you're old

2719. He has far too many conditions to experience unconditional love

2727. To achieve success, you have to be able to picture it realistically

2729. It's such a great feeling to give away something you love

2734. Some of these are pretty deep, which is surprising for such a shallow life

2740. You say things when you drink that you should probably say when you're sober

2746. If you have to claim you're an angel, it can't possibly be true

2751. What you think is irrelevant to how I feel

2756. If I remembered more than half the things I've done, I'd be twice who I am

2759. Once you enter the hospital, your chances of recovery are diminished

2765. Of course it's true, it came from her big book of meaningful assumptions

2773. The key to sucking your belly in is for it to actually look like you have abs

2777. I have a plausible solution to all of your serious objections

2779. Nothing better than to fart in a tuxedo and I know because I've worn one

2784. You're a really good observer but I want a participant

2786. We all get bad press, just different scales

2795. When we mess with a species, we always end with excess feces

2800. You can only have so many sessions without any progress

2807. An opportunity is only great if you do something with it

2812. To hell with the glass half full, I live by the 'ask for forgiveness' policy

2815. You can see well through my glasses but it's not the same as walking in my shoes

2821. If she'd only take off her defense, I'd raise my offense

2825. What does it matter if I cheat when I've already told you I lie

2829. I'm not well behaved but the best ones aren't

2835. Commitment fraught with problems is better than problems without commitment

2841. It's much better to have a plan and fail than to fail without one

2845. I live like I'm on the edge of the cliff, waving my arms backwards so I don't fall

2850. If it's not a problem for me now, it's pending

2860. I spend effort being good just so I can bank bad time

2868. I have a memory but it's just resting right now

2875. To improve your relationship, enjoy the sex you have or ask for what you want

2881. No upbringing is excellent

2885. If you're always late, never show up on time

2888. How do people who don't like to shop, shop for someone to shop for them

2890. Sorry, I'll shut up now but only for a short period of time

2898. Complaining about how your body looks is more unattractive than how you look

2900. I need therapy for a disorder that hasn't been discovered

2903. I listen to your words but pay attention to your actions

2906. I don't get mad, I just get more patient

2908. Make sure the smoke is thick enough before pulling out the mirrors

2914. There's a difference between keeping her happy and not pissing her off

2919. No better time for learning when faced with something you don't know how to do

2922. It's never those who provide the money who get blamed

2932. Clean up any failed relationships because they are a burden to carry

2937. You're so cute when you guess right

2941. Expect it to be difficult to deal with anyone you think is really smart

2947. I'm sorry, whatever your reason is, it doesn't work for me

2952. My aspiration is to be a mean statistical representation of my demographic age group

2959. The scariest part is trusting yourself

2965. That's only how you think you should behave because of what you were taught

2969. Since I'm unaware of the passing time when with you, you make me immortal

2974. Every day I'm the best I've ever been

2975. There's no value in trying to trace the origin of conversational tangents

2979. The only thing better than virgin olive oil is slutty balsamic vinegar

2984. Hope is the only stopper for a vessel of unrequited love

2988. You have to have courage and take risks to speak your mind

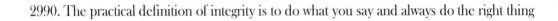

2990. The practical definition of integrity is to do what you say and always do the right thing

2996. By the way, you need a guy who takes risks

2997. If you don't want alcohol in your life, you shouldn't promote its use

3000. We fight others' problems every day so no need to run away when we have one

About the Author

Neil McClure was born in Denver, Colorado and grew up in Northern California. He holds degrees in Electrical/Electronic Engineering, Physics and a Master of Science in Systems Management. Neil began his professional career in the aerospace industry, doing 'rocket science' for a few years. He then moved on to the medical industry, working on devices for patient monitoring. From there, he launched into the entrepreneurial world, which has largely remained the focus of his professional pursuits until the present day.

Neil filed his first U.S. patent in December 1995 and now holds over 20 patents across a variety of industries and product types. Most notably was the creation of an electronic voting system that collected more than 15 million votes across the country in the 2016 Presidential election.

His current interests and product pursuits are in imaging processing, artificial intelligence, data analytics and GIS-based addressing. Neil currently has a variety of products and pending patents in play. In addition, he advises on technology strategy and product requirements for product development in a variety of industries.

Avid recreational interests include water skiing, snow skiing and (bordering on obsession) kite boarding. Neil primarily uses hot yoga and a little free-weight conditioning to maintain his weekend warrior status. He is in excellent physical condition, maintains that he is still reasonably attractive and, not to mention, very modest...

Neil married before graduating college, divorced, and cooperatively raised two children to adulthood who provide his greatest sense of accomplishment.

Made in the USA
Middletown, DE
02 September 2019